Free Verse Editions

Edited by Jon Thompson

CONTRAPUNTAL

Christopher Kondrich

Parlor Press
Anderson, South Carolina
www.parlorpress.com

Parlor Press LLC, Anderson, South Carolina, 29621

© 2013 by Parlor Press
All rights reserved.
Printed in the United States of America
S A N: 2 5 4 - 8 8 7 9

Library of Congress Cataloging-in-Publication Data

Kondrich, Christopher, 1982-
  [Poems. Selections]
  CONTRAPUNTAL / Christopher Kondrich.
     pages cm. -- (Free Verse Editions)
  Poems.
  ISBN 978-1-60235-367-1 (paperback) -- ISBN (invalid) 978-1-60235-368-8
(Adobe ebook) -- ISBN (invalid) 978-1-60235-369-5 (ePub)
  I. Title.
  PS3611.O58465C66 2012
  811'.6--dc23
                              2012044929

                          1 2 3 4 5

Cover design by David Blakesley.
Cover image: Robyn O'Neil, 'Staring into the blankness, they fell in order to
  begin." © 2008 by Robyn O'Neil. Used by permission.
Excerpt from "Napoleonette" from *The Little Door Slides Back* by Jeff Clark.
  Copyright © 2004 by Jeff Clark. Reprinted by permission of Farrar, Straus
  and Giroux, LLC.

Printed on acid-free paper.

Parlor Press, LLC is an independent publisher of scholarly and trade titles in
print and multimedia formats. This book is available in paperback and ebook
formats from Parlor Press on the World Wide Web at http://www.parlorpress.
com or through online and brick-and-mortar bookstores. For submission
information or to find out about Parlor Press publications, write to Parlor Press,
3015 Brackenberry Drive, Anderson, South Carolina, 29621, or email editor@
parlorpress.com.

Sometimes a ghost entered my heart and I could feel, and sometimes phrases entered my mind and I could speak, with reason. But never was I able to stay a man long enough to remain him.

— *Jeff Clark, "Napoleonette"*

Whatever we do on the piano is a collection of illusions.

— *András Schiff*

Contents

CONTRAPUNTAL

So I take my hand,
and even though I know my hand,
I know I know it,
it feels like your hand.
I take it but I'm tired.
I know I'm tired because I squeeze
what I see between my eyelids.
Then I dream that your mind is mine.
I dream that I secure it
with my end of the rope.
I wake while saying
that what I say is the truth,
that you should believe me
because I say it.

Book One

If there's one thing
I remember apart
from all other things,
that I remember it
is astounding to me
though maybe not
to Tim who I recounted
this to before I left,
I recounted that you
arrived home one day
fatigued as much as
I've seen anyone fatigued,
you could barely connect
to your life and in a way
you felt as though
it were repeating.

You were aware
that it repeated, but
you had no control,
all the little things
you did that day
were out of character,
you had been exposed
to T, the lab bustled
with dishes and you
wore the protective gear,
but you said perhaps
it wasn't enough,
there could be no
other explanation
for your fatigue,
there had been no out-of-
the-ordinary activity
besides working
with the dishes of T,
which were introduced
that day by members
of a parent company.

When they presented you
and your colleagues
with Petri dishes,
you felt a little uneasy,
but mainly because it
was something new,
not because the dishes
caused some red flag
to pop up, you always
tell me of your uneasiness
when something new
enters your life and
you haven't had what
you feel is enough time.

I feel it all the time
even now as I recall
the story I once told
Tim and see the path
up ahead that I'm
encountering now,
I haven't had any
time to prepare
unless you consider
the path I've taken
thus far as preparation,
but either way I can
empathize with you,
not to mention empathize
with myself as I felt
that day telling you
that I can because
I did at the time
and I do now.

I memorized the
melodies of the world,
played them back
as I was listening
to them in real time,
the twin melodies
were slightly off,
one was a bit ahead,
or maybe one was
a bit behind, I couldn't
tell, but this created
an echo that shared
as much of itself
with my ears as
it did its origin.

The melodies amounted
to gibberish, but gibberish
so close that I ascribed
words to it, so I could
take what I wanted.
The tree sang *soon*
the wind will blow
the leaves from me,
and the bushes rustled
remember, remember.
The tones of the day
were sustained so long
as I held my attention
up against them,
which wasn't easy,
I wanted and wanted
to fall into the soil.

I was always one for
decorum on an aural level,
but this was new, I was
able to put my suspicions
aside for the moment
and concentrate on
the pleasure of discord
for the first time,
which was the thrum
of opposing strings,
the sudden convulsion
of those strings against
the daylight reaching
the branches, finding
my eyes now closed,
telling me something
I would soon forget.

I came to an embankment
of geese, a startling number,
the vision of which was
strongest when I closed
my eyes. I saw the geese
with my ears, so to speak,
and I spoke with my skin—
the dream I was lost in.
The wind threw dust
off the pages of trees
up to where I stood near
the embankment of geese,
their image in my hands.
I listened to them
opening their beaks,
turning their heads, loud
as my pounding heart.
I watched them with a bit
of my own eyes, a bit
of yours that I had found
hidden in some straw.
They didn't stir apart from
their usual stirring or break
their gaze—it was as good
a time as any to be happy
with what was before me.

I decided to call Tim
and he picked up,
it had been so long,
his voice sagged
in my ears, I barely
caught the sound,
it sagged with age
and T like a branch
sagging with ice.
You have to believe
that it's really me
on the line.

My idea is a recital
of our thoughts because
thoughts are what make
a life worth living,
maybe the recital
should be in the field,
but we would have to listen
to the music apart
from what happened
up to that moment,
devoid of history,
personal or otherwise,
the stars would reveal
themselves a little
at first then all at once,
we'd be able to see them
as though they were inches.

I prepared for the recital
by clearing the path
of stray rocks, by
following my mind
like a nose from one
room to the next.
At times, I imagined
my suit walking around
without a body inside it,
just the suit by the window
trying to adjust its tie.

I waited until
I couldn't wait
any longer to ask
if you still planned
to join me, for so long
things were happening
but now nothing
was happening,
wind blew or didn't
through windows
I opened or closed.
I felt as though I were
staring at a camera.

Later, when I spoke
to the empty house,
I spoke about how
you were another person
entirely, which made me
think that there was
someone else who
might want to be me
as much as I did.

I was lost due to
some clerical error,
and I walked a path
I made for myself
looking back every
so often to see
if there wasn't
something I missed,
but I hadn't missed
anything there was
only an expanse
up ahead that
didn't seem so grand
until I reached up.

I felt no air
from the blades,
but a helicopter
dangled its ladder
above my hands,
I didn't know I had
to look for it or that
it would be waiting
for me, the ladder
was an epiphany,
and when I entered
the body of the helicopter,
I found it unmanned
except for me and
the switches.

I peered down at
the spot where I was
just a moment ago,
and I remembered
how the ground felt,
and how the wind
caught my attention,
then flitted off to rustle
some shrub or stem,
I moved by losing interest,
propelled forward
by the need to find
another spot where
I could settle, call you
and say I'm somewhere
I know nothing about.

The wind had two layers,
carried itself on its back,
I tried to remember more,
but it dispersed before
I could give it an outline,
a shape. My day was spent
looking around for something
to take for granted, because
rediscovering is sometimes
more rewarding than what is
rediscovered. The weather
did not cooperate, it jabbed
its rainy fingers against the
windows, the rest of the day
waited, its thinking reeds ready
to sway with the current,
to point up as I hovered
over them able to bend.

The second time
I hovered over
the field I was
able to touch down,
I hesitated at first
then flew off just
in case there
was another field
just like this one,
but it was the
right one and
I had no doubt,
when I saw
the house for
the second time,
I knew it was the
right spot, I heard
a melody inside
that I loved.

I should've
assumed the shape
of an obstruction
since that is the shape
a love object takes
when it blots out
what is beyond it,
and there is nothing
else in one's visual field,
but I was alone to
crest the forest, to
touch down slowly
and see the air
from my propellers
comb the tall grass
all in one direction
just as I had always
wanted to comb grass,
I would daydream
about it, my eyes
would gloss over
the newspaper.

You couldn't sleep,
your life was fatigue
in the way the life
of an eye is what it sees,
and you worried about it,
which made it worse,
you worried about being
worried, which made it
worse and it consumed
your waking thoughts,
which were beginning
to take on the attributes
of your dreams if you
could remember their
attributes correctly,
you walked the dishes
of T around the lab
with your hands in
the same position.

You had taken T
thinking it would
help you sleep
after a long day
in contact with it,
but that was counter-
intuitive I said,
T cannot be the
source of your
sleeplessness and
what puts you to sleep,
that which causes
sickness cannot cure,
I said sounding
all of my years
even though I wasn't
that old I felt older
than I was, and
I peered at my
reflection in the window,
I was young
but getting older
by the minute, getting
older without you.

Book Two

We have a problem here, Tim said tossing his coat
over the back of the couch. You seem to think

> with exactitude on this matter, more so than I can
> Tim said, surveying the empty chairs

with such overwhelming joy and sadness
for this strange instrument

> because what we seek whether we admit it or not
> is our destruction, or that little bit of doubt that builds character

when I play, I hear only one note
perhaps this is because I have tuned the piano that way

> I hold the piano up to my ears to hear
> its chest empty each time I touch it

in the morning I go to sleep at night
knowing that I will be there when I awake

> I live alone and I've shored up my house
> with all the things that were lying around.

That beautiful melody? It is already within us
Tim was sorting through his compositions

    we need to find a way to bring it closer
    to brush our end against its end, but we must remain

and regardless if I am satisfied
I have to abide by the metronome

    I want to study piano because in doing so I will destroy
    my discreteness. One is always concerned with one's discreteness

this tiresome harangue of mine
just as I was reaching the terminus or whatever point

    in the mind that receives it. Listen to this, Tim said
    playing nothing. Do you hear what I hear

I have to do it myself
with my own hands

    sometimes I am struck, my chair a closer
    companion than anyone I know.

I raised my hand, but he didn't call on me
he talked about how, in the future, we'll all get what we want

      to other cupboards. Needless to say, everyone in that house
      suffered. Why am I telling you this

as though I were transmitting information over a short distance
when you first told me you didn't want me to play

      into the void, what were you going to do
      about it?

I told you something like this was going to occur
just at the moment when I was about to conclude

      this starting point
      we need the struggle, Tim said

but I'm telling you that this is entirely false. It's a delusion
you've cooked up. I remember

      falling through is always on my mind and the keys
      receive this worry with every touch.

It was a relief to hear it said, I had always worried about that
but somewhere along the line we'll have to

> and the part of you that functions has to search constantly
> for the things it needs to put dinner on the table

to get a clear picture
of our auditory field

> the form of one's life, Tim said, is unceasing motion
> and yet you've somehow mistaken stagnancy for motion

during this supposed recital, I was skeptical and still am
now where is that piano of yours

> I don't know why I said there was one to begin with
> but this is the issue—using words that capture

each day has triggered this delusion. Maybe T has tricked you
into thinking that the house you return to each night

> was listening. Maybe that job
> has screwed something up.

To be absorbed, which is what I want—to be absorbed into the world
I'll play the music that calls to you, that is calling your name

       that would justify me sticking my neck into the void
       and shouting to the nearest person, Hey, my neck is sticking

the older I got, the more emphatic the voice became
then I understood. I don't know how, but I did

       in order to have purpose. Sometimes we need to dash
       ourselves on the rocks because the reassembling

the thrashing or burning rids
the next day of having to decide

       in there, Tim said knocking my head with his fist
       when I was a child I used to think I wasn't real

but I thought if I could hear a longing and lilting melody
in one note, I could hear anything

       I don't want to depress you, so let's just say there's a method
       and leave it at that.

Tonight, the piano will project me into a dream
in which I'm on stage. It's a terrible night

      to discover what we were composed of. Without first
      breaking, Tim said, we can't be whole

be threaded outside into something wonderful
and this is called counterpoint

      a need to return to a previous state
      buried beneath years of habit and rationale

even when I was already there
there was a voice inside me

      make some sacrifices—this includes sacrificing what we want
      because once we have it, we become different people

completely separate and meaningful
which is to say that whatever is inside us

      hope it will allow
      the mistakes I know I will make.

I won't say Bach or Schoenberg; I'll say that I am my favorite composer
because I believe I would make the same choices

      as that one day, I don't remember its qualities or weather
      but you advised me

without touching the piano
we can listen to our elements

      our thoughts and intentions correctly, but also with the right tone
      maybe there's someone else in this room who can speak

this forward motion into direction itself
a method to sustain us

      whether or not
      I have to make this decision

in the last row, I felt as though I were sitting
on the bench next to him. That's how he played

      that's what one of your colleagues asked me
      the man asked me if I felt looped.

How am I supposed to go about loving someone
more than this chair when its legs wobble

      for fear of what it would shrink into. I only want to recall
      when I had some whiff of the future

you have to overlook what brings about understanding
because it doesn't matter. I understood my need

      and even if I wanted it destroyed
      I'd have to decide beforehand to do it

I have always wanted to go home, Tim brooded
it was the last time I saw him before he tucked away

      the blandest of foods
      our tiny mirror

the keys on a piano are struck separately
the future is full of music

      ladies and gentlemen, Tim said though it was only me
      we have an epidemic in this country.

Book Three

As I walk through the door to the lab, I am continuously repositioned before the threshold.

I am stuck in a loop of taking the first step en continuously repositioned before the doorway, before the separation of hallway and lab. This loop feels not unlike a dream, one that persists right before waking, in the tier of consciousness directly below consciousness, below the surface where light is redirected.

I am able to remember how the wool of my sweater chafes a bit of skin on my wrist, my left wrist where the cotton shirt that buffers my skin from the wool has ridden up, the glow and hum of halogen lights

a paler shade, a paler light than the more yellowish light of the hallway.

I hear one of my colleagues say my name in recognition. My ear admits the sound before it echoes against the wall. How strange it would be for him to see me in this loop   crossing and re-crossing the threshold unless his experiences are also looped but in a way applied especially to him. He sits perpendicular to my line of sight and is thus suspended in my periphery

                              which is then taken from me, I am stripped of my periphery each time I am repositioned and each time I obtain visual and auditory information.

I'm not able to piece together the information because each piece is the same shape, same size, but how often do you gain knowledge with the same contours and dimensions multiple times, how often can you examine the knowledge you gain and its duplicates, how often are its copies laid out before you.

I was about to put a check mark next to the name on my list of the patient who I just met with.

I remember how much I love checking off a name on my list, not to mention how lovely the check mark is, with its two lines perpendicular to each other and turned on their side whereas each of the lines contain a little of the ink from the other line from the moment the pen hesitates.   T was administered to eight chimps and we tested their response to a jaguar,

which acted like a wall or rather was itself a wall erected to quarantine fear to an inaccessible sector of the brain and when

the chimps weren't afraid, we did tests on the jaguar to see if aggression was effected

species to species. I wrote a report on ivory-colored paper of a high stock, it all looked very nice, the lettering, the paper, it was all very professional, but it was too late, the parent company had begun general production.

The vials
and, therefore, their contents, had typeface that softened the corners
of the world just enough so you could go about your day without
anything coarse rubbing against you, without one thing or another

slipping into pockets of the mind.

The vast majority   did not consider the label with any depth,
they only had a perfunctory understanding of the label because, as
one of the provided choices stated,   the text seemed *familiar
in a way that [they couldn't] put [their] finger on.*

T could have side effects the parent company imagined, effects that were rooted in the part of the brain that would do such imagining,

though this was all conjecture, conjecture until it became rumor, rumor that was met with ambivalence

because of the perceived benefits.

If by fracturing we mean release, one columnist speculated, *perhaps it is for the best. Yes, this could mean the opportunity to view*

as others do.

I, for one, hope this occasions a view
upon which we can all agree.

I remember pointing to the graphs with my red laser, directing attention from one part of the graph to another by moving the red dot of the laser from one area to another,

the laser pointer moved with the content of my speech as the content shifted, the hand that held it was given commands from the central command of my mind, my mind gave the command to move the laser pointer at the very same moment

                                                    I was shifting topics,
the topic did not precede the command, which is the way the mind operates, it is able to preempt the shifting content of its thoughts with the intended action,

it is so wonderful for my mind to speak of this as my body is reminded again that circumstance is king, that it commands the body in the same way I commanded my hand.

We didn't know exactly what we were looking for, we didn't know how the abnormality would present itself, in what sector, in what form, on what day—

this was after months of finding nothing.
We believed one man in particular presented his story in a unique manner, the man's story was such an extraordinary one that for the first time in months we honestly expected to find evidence in the scan, but I was there for the man's story and didn't find it noteworthy in the least.

At one time,
we thought that since so much is still unknown, there could be bat-
tlegrounds. We also went so far as to speculate that these areas of the
brain could also be where the [force of instinct and desire] resides,
which is to say that one could believe anything and still find a rela-
tionship between what one believes and T.

One man admitted that T made him feel.

He began to study piano, obsessively study piano to the extent that he took T thinking it would improve his playing,

and even though it didn't improve his playing, he didn't have any psychological troubles either, he experienced some looping, but looping is to be expected when playing the piano,   there are melodies that recur, sometimes in a minor key, sometimes at an increased tempo and you have to keep up with the melody or what's the point,

one has to keep at it until it is played not only with perfection, but also with emotion, emotional rigor he called it, rigor of emotional expression, rigor in form and timing, he told us.

I remember cleaning out my desk, rearranging my things

in a cardboard box, so a dish could fit in this one, thin crevice.
I was trying to guess the time, trying to see if what I felt the time
was, was in fact the correct time when a colleague came up to me and
wanted to know if we had similar notions.

Faint, comfortable smiles on my colleague's face and the faces of the
men at the door who carted a tray of dishes so flimsy in my hand, I
was afraid I was going to spill it, but I didn't spill it,
I put one hand underneath it.

Time has oxidized to a dull green. Those given a placebo have experienced the same psychological side effects—

a collective expression of certain anxieties that have been, perhaps, dormant.

I am one of these participants, but only time will tell if it's really me, the time it takes to walk through the door to the lab, over the threshold and back before the threshold, the time that is actually progressing, the past, moving forward, piecing together the present, moving forward for as long as I can remember.

Book Four

Lying awake
I heard two voices
both of which were mine.
I was always afraid they
would remove what I held
in my invisible hands,
and then came the hour
I had to accept
because living meant
accepting the loss
of one hour after another,
or what felt like an hour,
which could be two,
which could be none,
a mere few minutes
compressed into a rock
the size of a thumb.
I spent part of the night
on the couch another part
at the kitchen table—
I would like some tea,
said one of my voices.

You can't resolve any issue
at this time of night,
no one is at their phone,
waiting for your breath
in the receiver. The hand
over your heart will not
slow the beating, neither will
the memory of that one day
you thought there was something,
that you forgot what it was,
but you were wrong.
If only you could recapture
the absence you felt that day,
swollen with forgetfulness
but hopeful. If only you
could open an umbrella
inside your chest, you'd
have room for something else.

We need the mind to know
our weight, Tim said, without it
we'd have no way of knowing.
We shouldn't do what we can
to contain it, we should release it,
and you know what they say
about things that don't return.
Maybe a tenuous grasp is
enough to remain comfortable,
and isn't retaining comfort
a pleasure in itself? You can't,
Tim said, force a picture into
a frame, and even if you could,
the picture would regard it as
an extension of its landscape.

Because the body is an
anchor I want a house
in the middle of a field
where the road that leads
in is the road leading out,
a place where I participate
in some unusual wonder
that lasts beyond mention
beyond reason, each day
the grass sways with it,
and I stay in that field
night arrives and I stay
in that field peering up
into the mind inside
the mind, then I shift
in value depending on
who thinks of me who
thinks ill of me.

He was in the process
of arriving for a while,
his hat arrived,
then some trinkets
I assumed were his,
and when I asked him
about the trinkets
he said he didn't know,
someone else must have
assumed they belonged here,
and then he dismissed me
the way one dismisses
another when one is tired
of everything always
being around.

Having recalled
what Tim said,
I hoped to hear
the same sounds,
the murmuring
that displaced me
then, but would
settle me now
because your voice
would be here
when the body
of you couldn't.
I tried to conjure
your image that
I hold in my mind,
but nothing came,
there was a path
circling the house
that wasn't going
to walk itself.

I was making headway
though I knew not how.
I was gaining ground
by losing it. Ahead
was what lay beyond,
and behind was where
I'd been. There were
mountains that hovered
in the west and east
under muted stars,
communicating with
melody, which sent
chills, tired and small.
The point that shown
through the fog was
where my things were.
I had left them ahead
so I had some clothes
and soap where I was
going to rest each night.
I heard a strong wind
shove aside the breeze—
it was a good thing
I brought some T.

Tim was taking T
to help his fingers
move over the keys
with more agility,
he said that the
specks of dust
that collect on the keys
he rarely strikes
drifted differently
when he dusted them
than the specks
of dust that collected
on the stack of compositions
he rarely plays, yes
he said, there are two
modes of drifting since
there are two separate
locations from which
the specks drift.

I didn't know that
he was taking it
to improve his playing,
this was an area of
Tim's life that was
firmly linked to routine,
any new variable
could throw off
his routine even if
this new variable was
meant to benefit it,
I'm sure there were
clues along the way
I would've picked up
on if I were paying
closer attention, but
I've been preoccupied,
I've been staring
at a green coat
in a room with many
of our friends without
regard for how they
got there or when
they were going to leave.

Though you must linger
until I send for you,
know that there's poetry
in the purgatory you keep.
The house may be quiet,
but there is much to do
that you couldn't when
I was there. The lab needs
you—they wouldn't have
called as much as they did.
I had a pretty good day,
I suppose—it was nothing,
until I found a chair
in the middle of it.
This is where I'm sitting.
I've come to think of the world
as the mind's refrain,
synthesizing what we've done
and seen, but succinctly,
so that we can remember
as the days become day.

I'm not there yet, nor
do I know how long it'll
take to arrive. In fact,
I won't know I've arrived
until I have. This self-
sustaining logic, though
frustrating, is the only
way I convey truthfully.
Anyway, can logic even
have truth? Only to the
extent that what it proves
is truthful. Do you agree?
I'm not saying you have to,
but knowing that you do
is knowing that you're with me,
that, at this point along the way,
you are here, too.

What was disappointing
was not that the recital
was over, but that Tim
hadn't chosen the right
piano, he immediately
expressed his concern,
but I told him the piano
hadn't been in use,
it had just sat there,
but he said that that
was precisely the reason
why the right piano
had to be chosen to sit
beside us the whole time,
its immobility was itself
a great accompaniment—
that the right piano
wasn't chosen was a
blackness that shrouded
us, a woolen pall.

You have to choose
the right piano for
the right composer,
in this case we are
the composers, so the piano
shouldn't have been
a Steinway, it is clear
in my mind that Steinway
was the obvious but not
correct choice, with its
responsiveness to major
concertos, to Bach, but
not to us, we should've
gone with a Bösendorfer
or something more inclined
to our condition, more
like the condition of our
shadows. I want to return
to when the choice
of piano was before me.

If I chose the Bösendorfer,
I would now be saying
that the Steinway was
the obvious choice,
that I was a fool
to pass up what was
clearly the optimal piano—
this is the real problem,
now we are getting
at the real issue …
I don't play the piano
for its repertoire,
I play for its closeness—
the music is always
so close to my hands,
I can feel the sounds
between my hands
as I clasp them to play.

Perhaps we were led
astray by our inclinations
towards a Bösendorfer
or Steinway when our
real answer was a
Schimmel all along,
but I detest the Schimmel
with its indeterminateness
and squeaking wheels.
I remember the one
Schimmel I played
when I was a child—
it kept shifting
when I struck the keys.
I was told I was
frustrating the instrument
with pent up suffering.
I was an emotional child,
crying at every turn,
and my hands were
such an extension of this
emotion that when
I frustrated the instrument,
as I was told, the wheels
squeaked with its movement,
which is why, in this case,
I was so immediately
deterred by the Schimmel
that I gravitated towards
the Steinway and Bösendorfer
and swung between them.

In Beethoven's time,
in Vienna, there were
more than one
hundred piano makers,
each with their own
inclination towards
one sound or another,
the choice could've
been even harder,
the sheer number
of pianos would've
made choosing one
an impossibility.
Our choice was
simple by comparison,
if we cannot choose
between a Steinway
or Bösendorfer, how
will we ever choose
anything else? This
is the path we create,
the one that pieces
us together into one man
or another, the piano,
or the one fixing his
pant leg, shaking it
to get the creases out.

I couldn't dawdle.
I had a few things
I wanted to do before
the day was over.
I was always so adamant
that I perform certain duties,
I couldn't finish
the day and move
onto the next one
until these minor tasks
were completed and
I had checked them
off my mental list,
my aria, which,
in its reoccurrence,
brings melody to me
on its schedule, the sound
of my absence, of all
absence, as I check
off, item by item,
what anchors me
to this world.

We have a greater capacity
for knowledge and
a greater capacity
for pain, I said to Tim,
a capacity that's awkward
and cumbersome and
never full even when
it's bored out of its mind.
I wasn't going to say
it again and then I did,
I said it and saw the air
outside wafting against
the window like the breath
of a dog waiting for me, waiting
for something I would do
to make us both so certain
that the trees and sky
were there, were ours.

Acknowledgments

Grateful acknowledgment is made to the editors of the following publications, where portions of this poem—some under a different title and in a slightly different form—first appeared: *Bombay Gin*, *Boston Review*, *Cimarron Review*, *Free Verse*, *Meridian*, *Notre Dame Review*, *Painted Bride Quarterly*, *RealPoetik*, *Sonora Review*, *Swink*, *The Journal*, *Witness*, *Yemassee* and *Zone 3*. Additional acknowledgement is made to *Verse Daily* for featuring a selection on their website.

Thank you, Timothy Donnelly, for your encouragement, wisdom and friendship. This book would not have happened if not for you. Also, thank you Eleni Sikelianos, Mark Strand, Mark Svenvold and Bin Ramke for your endless support and guidance.

I am also extremely grateful to Jon Thompson and Parlor Press.

This book is for Michelle, and for my parents.

Index of First Lines

About the Author

Christopher Kondrich is a PhD candidate at the University of Denver and an editor for *Denver Quarterly*. His poetry has been published in *American Letters & Commentary*, *Barrow Street*, *Boston Review*, *Cimarron Review*, *Free Verse*, *Meridian*, *Seneca Review*, *Verse Daily* and elsewhere. He lives in Denver.

Photograph of the author by Dan Cordle.
Used by permission.

Free Verse Editions

Edited by Jon Thompson

www.ingramcontent.com/pod-product-compliance
Lightning Source LLC
Chambersburg PA
CBHW032026090426
42741CB00006B/745